Pericopes

Pericopes

Miles Groth

ENI Press
New York, NY

ISBN 978-0-692-64842-1

for BC

Contents

Short Poems and Lyrics

Mothers and Fathers

New York Poems

Visions

Pericopes are cuttings and so are always items taken out of context. Sometimes, however, cuttings are sources of new growth when single stems with ragged ends are placed in a new medium, form roots, and grow over time into something full and whole. Most turn out to be merely ornamental and are destined for their opening and a short life. They provide some color and hasten to a dessicated demise.

Archibald MacLeish wrote to me that he hoped to leave behind a few poems that would be hard to get rid of. These *pericopes* will likely be easy in the going away, and since they have now been cut away from me, I have no more say about them.

A number of these cuttings are about boys, a group who are having a renaissance of interest everywhere. Like cuttings they have always had a hard time of it and deserve some special attention.

All of these are love poems since each was written with someone in mind.

They were written from the early 1970s on.

New York, 2016

Brothers, Boys, Men

GIACOMETTI'S BROTHER

All my life, Diego,
I've turned the same young form between my fingers:

dusky, somber, tenuous lines of life,
your body's long, invisible lines of heat.

I worked slight streaks into bronze flesh,
stringent, compelling metallic strength,
still, as slight as memory.

All my life, Diego,
I've worked your face with a feathery brush

to shape your shadowed eyes.
I draw around one finger
the ring that marries you to your smile.

MILD WHITMAN BOYS

Boys of all ages
parading that they are
play out the specimen beauty
of a long-forgotten shame.
Contemplable untouchables
walking in tense iconic isolation,
they pose even in motion
defined by a mechanical precision.
Who are their never-ending, all-defining judges?
Who demands their immaculate self-conception?
Why their bodies' sad execution?

COMING TOGETHER

Coming days without gender
grow under the blacklight of boys.
Puer rises at night
like the ever undead
dark side of the scaling moon.
An end to twinning
brings us together.
Nature heads to a stranger new union.
We two unwind history
back to the mind of God,
as Hegel thought it was
before there was time.

SHORTY KNOWS

A blonde, second-grade Pan in training,
Shorty never rests.
He enters rooms backwards,
eyes rolling epileptically ceilingward.

Shorty never sleeps.
At night, he roams alone
at loopy mosquito speed
deserted spots
and dark-eyed streets.
A true city Puck,
he makes dust whorl
at the corners.

Exhausted by seven years of his delight,
Mother knows better
than to look him in the face.
Long since dead
from smiling back,
she's learned to watch him in a mirror.

An older taller boy
with long impassive face
comes brothering him around the corner,
offers his hand for slap practice,
buys him a slice, calls his bluff,
holds his hand like a lover.
They cross at Charles Street,
nowhere to go on a thick, close
July Village night.

Shorty never smiles.
No need to be happy
when one sees things
no other needs or wants.

Shorty stands up to gravity,
and where he's still
the orientation of Earth is nonsense.
He knows the position we are in.
Shorty knows.

THE SWAN BOY OF JACKSON SQUARE PARK

I saw him first as he came to rest,
crazy-feathered,
beside five sweating homeless men,
pigeons devouring rodenticide,
the neighborhood transgendered sunning themselves,
and the one remaining butterfly
below Central Park.
Amid sheets of wind-ripped, airborne *Times*
he settled like calm
over an ageing woman.

In prep-school uniform
white socks furled to the ankles,
a huge pink shirt
loose and open all night,
thick brown Holden hair,
he had a once-trashed copy of *Catcher*
tucked under his wing.
But preferring to *be* the book,
he kissed it on the spine
and made a nest of pages torn
from its moist insides.

A gawky Plisetskaya,
the kid drew up one leg,
then another under,
pulled it all together —
book, head, wings, pigeons, me —
and like a dying swan
reposed in alert avian sleep.

Over the edge of a Wyeth field,
his singing wove the waving rye
and dreamed him through
its long oneiric drift.
He shocked awake and shook his head
like a rain-drenched spaniel.
Wind from the Hudson
unerringly parted his hair midline.
He stretched and yawped
a gullish silent howl aloft,
and something vivid summoned.

L-TRAIN DRUMMER

Every-day improvisation,
rave and rage
deafen skinny jazz boy.
Little by little
he hears less
as I see more
of his smiling duet
with noise and L-train ozone.
He riffs a banging chant
of ruckus on buckets
and one dismembered drum.
Everyone cheers.
He touches sticks,
flicking cues of freedom.
"I am who I am!"
he shouts at the tracks,
nervous, pale, alive since the 60s.
Tick-a-tick, tick-a-tick,
tick-a-tick – ah – *ah* – ah – bam!

I want to live his life.
Where does he feed?
Where does he roost
when the girls have gone
and ageing hippies in blues attire
hold their wondering in check?
Tick-a-tick, skinny stick,
tick-a-hit, tick-a-tick – ah ah *ah* – bam!

There is no underground to join
your jive to my travel,
your age to my lines,

no bridge to ease across the difference,
my pale, shocky son.
Tick-a-tock, tick-a-tick,
take-a-hit, take-it-back – ah *ah* ah – bam!

FOR ALL THE WORLD

For all the world,
he looked like he was hanging
on a cross: arms akimbo,
draped across the back
of a plastic bench,
his girl at right angles to him
twisting his hair
between gentling fingers.
Suddenly his head slumped forward
over the meager chest.
His legs turned in unison
from side to side
as she tried to contain him,
first with words,
then with wishes.
His body spoke assent.
His eyes, now closed,
said nothing.
He seemed to be dying,
I tell you,
in some unfamiliar way.
As she leaned in further,
her whirling hair
threw small shadows across his lap.
Each time a shadow struck
he shook in fearful exaltation,
concealing small messages.
At last, his joints gave way.
His silent places spoke
and like some broken dragonfly
by a western Pennsylvania country pond,
weakened by light and heavy air

and bound to a short life,
he pulled the gray hoody
over his head,
ready now to die,
fell off the rackéd rood,
snapped but saved,
and broke nature's promise.
A wish had put him there.

WHAT A LOOK IN THEIR EYES REVEALS

fastdraw
toughguy
sneerdrawl
hardwon
manhood

loveyou
fearme
faroff
longpass
heartthrob

can'ttell
won'ttell
makeme
tryme
daddyfrown

hideout
treehouse
loverboy
pipsqueak
superman

shameless
softplace
roughshake
knockdown
tenderloin

nighttime
wrongtime
dreamdrawn
moshdrunk
hotrodder

dareme
scareyou
jocktang
ruggedtone
starfire

looselimbed
hunchheavy
spitfire
redragged
breakdancer

longpass
sharpshot
moonstruck
mummy'sboy
conman

hapless
dadless
hatless
homeless
cowboy

February 21, 1999

HANDFUL

"He's a handful!" she yammered as he twisted
and shouts shocked his three-year-old frame
undone by unminding delays,
the rush and crush and push to sit
of rude shuffles and elbows,
a bewildering race,
even for a little boy.
He raged to ten thousand feet,
yelling at thunderheads,
getting redder on ascent.

"Sit still!" implored Mama,
ordering feeling to stop.
His screams chilled bad coffee.
Turned outside in,
he raged and raved
and danced on his back.

"Holy terror!" she murmured
in disgust of his little strength,
boy will and arching back,
as tears poured out
like unwanted rain
on a humid day.

"What does he want?" asked dads
fore and aft,
unable to cry with him.

Nothing worked:
not wordy cajoling,
deft baby cooing,

bribes and confessions,
threats' desperate measures,
and thoughts of a smothering.
Good-enough mothering
and seminar knowing —
all came to nothing.

But what she forgot
was his being a boy,
a lapful of tenderness
with a screaming heart.

Delta Flight 1160, Halloween 1999

THAT MOTHER

When that mother hit her son
dead center,
the heel of her hand
dislodged a million stars.
All fifty pounds of reeling shame,
his wren-bone chest held fast,
perhaps from practice,
but the blow done broke his heart to shatters,
made him first a hater,
then a sadder boy forever.
The fierce, deep breath he drew
held back one tear,
just one he kept for her
who drove him out and took away his home.
Later on his feet,
from there on out
young wide-eyed Oedipus
was on his own.

February 17, 2000

NIGHT CRAWLERS

One night ago like this,
weather-heavy with meteors
before the weather was numbers,
we lay for hours on the grass
waiting for just one brief burning to open up,
one rare streak of moon
like the luck of being a child.
Finally it came,
as unforgettable as the longest
thunderstorm on record in town,
the real first coming,
and what's immemorial
in Greensburg, Pennsylvania.

But I was getting to worms,
those thick spies from earth
that follow heavy rain
after a day of heaving storms
made the neighbor's brick (exactly like ours)
glow painterly sunburn red at six o-clock or seven.
We gathered them for fishing.
It meant the treat of staying up late,
walking softly, slowly,
reaching for the languid one,
absent-minded,
something dark emerging from dark,
swelling like the ground itself,
free in the open (it thought) to stretch
and safe at last from sun and shame,
reaching up, searching.

But for what?
Just to be caught?
It knew the robins were asleep.

We had all seen the few unlucky ones
caught at dawn,
no chance to escape by water
under cover of night.
Washed out of our yards,
beached on the scarred asphalt
of McArthur Street,
too far from saving cover,
barely distinguishable from twigs,
dessicated spaghettis for hungry swallows
who arrived at dusk.

If I held it long enough
and didn't pull too hard,
it came free
from a subterranean someplace
deep in the turf on which
all cows are dark.

I had it handily and held on to one—
"Got it!" I whispered—
eased it out gently, careful
not to tear the slimy thing
from its tendency to hide,
stay deep and fast,
unconnected in truth to anything
but rooted all the same somehow
in everything.

MEN IN TEARS
To Rip Torn

Striven de-
   livered
      riven
cut loose
   bentborn
            straightened
         shapeshifted
               drawn and
   singled ...
         mohel wounded
      un-
informed ...
         reformed
            fired upon
by bodysavors
      sawsought
            suddenly sexed
                  for facescraping delight ...
woman-handled
         pumped
            for spurtseed ...
benchchained desknailed
            hapless ...
                  or, soldierly, scalped
      to deliver Promethean
               firepower
or mere fodder,
         snipered
               cut open
      then pieced
            together ...

soldered
        till death
                breaketh him
from his other —
      or so they part,
            passing on
arid land
      hands cracked ...
the wildness
    gone to bewildered
         dying
in a wilder mess
    of tears
         shredded
from him ...
      then covered and kilned.

TO THE *RAGAZZI*

who show us how to leave a room without a trace
  owing it nothing

  modestly forgotten
  gaunt-shy

who know how to turn with the opening door
  releasing joy

  first-light flat
  translucently thin

who leave it to us to find the way to sorrow
  humoring us

  shadowly indifferent
  sec

who find everyone alone
  filling us with magic

  with much of nothing
  void's fullness

who give nothing to air's heaviness
  pressing us back

  head-tossing
  love smirking

who run their own way
  drawing lightning

messaging all night
barely of hints

who make up moments of solitary finds
abounding

one-time-only seen
first-person singulars.

THE LADS' PRAYERS

- I -

Fathers art in heaven.
They are not here.
Where the hallowed are they, then,
who wordless merely
came and went, and left
in moistrous royal chambers
and millions' kingdoms come
a single son behind?
Why will be anything done,
when none on earth
is ever man enough
or, better, bigger than a prayer?
No, let me start again. Amen.

- II -

Our father's art and name
are nothing if he a faceless donor be
to milky sopor frothed
and spent for lady's later buying
saying: "Let me pat it, pet,
to pleasure's end.
You've done so well,
you willowy son.
Thy willy be won, the little one,
on earth as if it were so heavenly.
Ah, what a good small boy you've been!
Stand up, little man."
No, let me surely start again. Amen.

Give us a way, you daily dread,
to save us this May
from deathly beds
of luscious daffodils.
And sing, for you suffer.
I hear it in your groans,
the little death.
Give it like a man and all will be forgiven,
as we forgive the dead
who said they'd make us better.
The lads, without a prayer,
forever. Amen.
No, I will not start again.

FOUR WAYS

i. vena basilica

The hand's one way
drains daydreams
from its fingers'
pause and wishes.
The beating heart
is far from known
to the drumming palm,
its course and pulse.

Hard pressed
to feel its source,
enclosing, webbing
a trembling fist,
it sells the soul
for a well-made arm.
The ventral smoothness
of a blood-route's bed
betrays the limits of bone.
Terror curls and presses
where sleep roamed
an hour ago.

Learning the way of the shaken hand,
the pinch and probe and wary slip
of too much lingering,
the strum of handling, holding,
petting, figuring,
beckoning, embolding
hard lessons leave behind their traces
on a prominent way

thickened by brushing hair
and stroking touch,
the signature of strength,
begotten of pleasure.

A hand pulls back the hood
and grasps and groans in solemn tones.
The sacred aperture opens, shy to praise.
Way of the royal house of Alexander,
you are the archon, prince and emperor
of choice and treasure,
and ore-stream of the Nile.

ii. vena cephalica

Topped taut ridgerunner
east of the heart
just under the edge of dominance,
swollen from climbing
the overbrimming emblem of manness
carved from headwater
and moves bravely made,
it aims for the chin
and points to the mouth
to say "I cannot speak,
feed me, crawl inside
the darkened word."

iii. vena jugularis externa

The short answer to old men's rages
is the first to speak in infant screams.
The way shows strain and flow,
an urge below, a tide of grins.

Crying's fluent icon,
the tanned prominence of boy-pleas
and tamed seductions
is free of recollection.

Now appears the broad rack
and wingspread proudly splayed.
See the mark of how he spoke and swore,
a boy who took his grinning power seriously.

In sudden breach of early bright
before the slay, it arched its back
and like the hump of a heel-gashed worm
it shook, engorged, and gasped.

This is the path from ear to throat,
pumping rhythmic eye-thoughts
to the heart's own well-known
Pascalian reason.

Consider its rushing speech and serpent mark.
The silence men perform,
their birdy spread and wingless flight,
the late or never smile,
shame's standard syllables,
and underground, the stream
heads north to Orion.

iv. *vena saphenica magna*

As rarely seen as touched,
it peeks below the gymnast's splay,
the vaulter's launch,
a freestyle flutter, the dancer's thrust.

This is the way that drain the toes,
the scarry knees, the boggy thighs.
Upward bound,
it strains to the trivium
of desire, wetness and waste.
Converging deep in love's body,
losing face,
an off-course root
briefly out of its depth,
the inverted why spits out imperatives
where body meets desire
in chemical devotion,
urge and submission.
The softest place to write about
is where the groaning hums
that mimics pain,
unsettles smiles,
and shows the underblush of joy,
relief and shame.

TO GUYS WHO HAVE NEVER GONE HUNTING

Set passion-deep
and made for roaming,
their hunter's eyes
are now the haunted eyes
of days near closing.

There in the glow,
dug deep and longing,
fire hides and burns its owners.

But will they see,
before time rounds the bend
and breaks their joy
and puts it down,
that love has made them,
like themselves, too little?

Or will they leave us there tonight,
all dulled and pointless
without their light,
to wonder just
what could have happened
if only they had not gone hunting?

NOTES FOR A POEM BY MICHELANGELO

Like every other maudlin,
I'm sure no one understands me
and yearn for transparency.
But I have made a calling of it,
a monastic habit.
Wanting something from one of these
boys I go in for,
out of my way for,
into the rain for,
is wanting to *have been* understood
at the nice, neat age of twenty.

I wanted someone
I could give things to.
This is what I was missing.
Requited love is willingness
to be at ease when gifted.

But now as then,
it's always the boys,
nothing given, nothing gained.
Maybe they sense
that when I look
I take something from them:
beauty, energy, desire.
This they do not want to share,
but since they cannot do without it,
nothing goes to me.

A WOMAN AND HER SHADOW

I first saw her lanky
no-nonsense hair,
tied close to flow long,
the girlish hair
of a tired, lopsided
middle-aged woman
with her teenage son.

She walked one step up,
another down,
as though with each
she jumped the curb
on a broken wheel.
With pained awkwardness
and already old for her years,
she refused his arm,
a shade darker than her face.
She never smiled.

And then I knew
the reason for her gait
and shadowing skirt
was his flawless, serious face.

August 23, 2000

Love Poems

TWO OF THEM

She saw his hiding secret sense
and smiled.
Out of sight,
he wouldn't blush.
That was his need.
Inviting his, her caution-starving patience
staving off the liquid creed
(waiting none the less) —
that was her gift
pleaded to him alone
to stay that way forever.
Could she make him smile?
A chance past banter
to bring him close
who wanted eyes
and nothing more.
Was that too little to dare,
to ask?

FOR RUMI AND SHAMS

He is the treasure,
She the vault.

She is the mouth,
he the breath drawn in.

She speaks. He goes out
like the last light

on his block in the middle
of her night.

She is the moving target,
he the arrow's sound

fired at dawn.
He is the prisoner who drops.

She is the reach,
he the arm.

He is the boy who ran away.
She stayed home.

He is the longing,
she the lure

that skims his stream
running east.

She is the sentence,
he the word not spoken.

He is the secret,
she the charm

hanging loosely around his neck,
the jewel on his throat.

She is the search,
he the thought.

She is the season,
he the angle of light.

She is the board,
he the game

played out in waning light,
in muffled sound.

He is the spoken line,
she the play.

He the living will, the testament,
she the legacy and love.

She is the window,
he the space

between the mountain
and table where she sits,

the view over the grass,
the scene she sets.

He is the missing chair,
she the broken door.

He is the swollen sash,
she the staring mirror.

She is the solemn shadow,
he the stain on the floor,

the burgundy mark
of her lover's blood.

She is the flowing air,
he the scent it carries.

She is the heavy pitcher,
he the empty glass

full of waiting,
rich with saving.

She is the signal to drink,
he the broken promise

she knew he would make
and pass along to others.

And when you close this book,
she is the page

and he the word
that she wrote down

to say that he was there
for her to tell:

"This poem wrote itself.
I never saw his face."

March 23, 2001

DEAR WALT

When Jack grasps Jill,
I'm there at the shoulder
that fits the palm,
or at the hip or mount
that fills the hand.

Not the curve, but the curving,
the weight, not the rest
we long for with scanning eye.

I cheer the falling forth
of every step,
all-precious balance
and the last-minute save.

I sing the seeking smile,
the closing eye,
the breathing bones,
the arching back.

It is the gesture we crave,
not the fact.

October 14, 2000

THE TABLE (I)

Tonight I spend the last currency
earned one evening months ago.
It ends now that time has been
all but swallowed down with cups
of Russian tea and springwater ice.

I already miss you
who conceived me a surprise on the grass
one summer afternoon out in the country.

Marvel me with your voice in this old house
and my story will tell
how the light in her kitchen
was oh so clear that night
around a table where Druids worshiped once.

You fashioned me
the ache another left behind,
and a bench on which to seat a constellation.
The evening was long.
The lines on Whitman's face wanted to be touched,
ageing lines like distant trees
guarding falling rain outside the window.

"Listen now, and hear the tap of twigs
laid side by side on a light branch," I said,
as your arm made a home on the table beside me.
Wrestle me with your eyes when I hesitate.
Press your face against the oak
where the world is only a disc
small ships forever falling off
lost for looking.

Call me friend finally
when it's later, closer,
to say how the summer went
when autumn and you together
were earth's one gender.

Last out the night.
The pause upon words makes little sense,
making me, in knowing you,
a welcome guest.

THE TABLE (II)

Your eyes blinked slowly.
Full night entered them,
all that remained of a bright day
still living in them.

They spoke, too, as your words
took on new life at the heavy oak table
we rested against
facing each other,
our arms just touching,
the near light of two small candles
pouring out in cupfuls onto my hands.

We talked of meeting another time
to play on earthy silt
when the moon washed the road
we sometimes walked along
all night together.

Then you leaned in to me
to better hear what I would not say,
and in that pressing summer air
I turned down my head
like a rain-soaked comfort
and began to dream
that only the season itself
could bear up my face
to look at yours again.

HOW I WOULD WALK UP TO YOU. WHAT I WOULD SEE. WHAT I WOULD SAY.

Your eyes are mythic,
wild and darting,
set pale in a face
already let go of innocence.
Those eyes that see mine
test my smile.

Crouched behind a dusty chair,
you know nothing of this,
the tested smile and nearing passion,
waiting without a way
to be sure just what I mean.

THE FIRST SUMMER

Your twentieth year will end tonight.
Today the sun stands still,
grows brighter.
You pass the pitched
tent of the earth.
A rare wide smile
ranges its limits across your face.
Houses you dreamed about
call you in to rest easy.

CUTTING LILACS

Let me put it this way:
When you're past your prime
and it's time for lilacs
the first warm day of the year,
call me long distance.

You'll narrowly miss me.
I'll be out with the cat,
cutting a bough to bring inside.
Ring ten times.
I'll miss you all the same.

IN THE GALLERY
Carnegie Museum, Pittsburgh

We decided to meet at the "Water Lilies."
I wondered how you would look
at the milky edge in that maze of galleries,
how your voice would sound in that light.
Would I know your footsteps there
where a camera shutter explodes?

It seems we talked together on that pond last year
drifting under the heavy sun,
and wondered how we would meet in a gallery
somewhere,
our contact hanging in the air like a painting
for questioning eyes and the relentless white surround.

Your staring eyes took the blue from hidden flowers
buoyed up by islet leaves
and steam as thick as heavy cream.

INCANTATION
for T.C.

I imagine my hands together on your chest
forming a closed bicuspid over your heart,
you standing there, tense,
touched by what haunts us both.

I write with the right
but think with the left,
and you at home under both
words and my thoughts.

I watch the rise and fall of your heart's bony cage
as it steadies, is regular, and rests.
I couldn't begin to imagine
my hands on the soft skin of your belly
with its flush of hair warding off
a stranger's gaze.

I am there not to be seen,
like the moon's other side
or the inward life.

March 3, 2002

M'AMUSE (ADMISSION, CONTACT AND PRAYER)

What I want from you —
manic, wonder-struck —
I finally admit,
is all I want for you:

loves of every kind
and a great heart,
as that Aristotle fellow had it;

your hand from time to time
plunged deep
into a mountain stream
like the one my father showed me once
that flows the same
no matter how cold the air
or warm the ground,
July or December,
year-round, always there,
always the same;

tenderness as touching
as that day in May
when you stretched your arm
across the vaporetto's comfortless backrest
and we so far from home;

and what speaks out
in tiny wordless, worrisome winks
(those grasping spasms around your eyes)
of someone who knows

but cannot say
what hit you one day
when you stood up to pray:

> Robbed of an easy god,
> make me a boy who knows
> what he may never have,
> and let me be as surely Yours
> as what You want from me.

July 25, 2003

INCIDENT IN VENICE

La Fenice had fallen again
into dusty dumbness.
I stumbled over your shadow
along the Lido.
Nothing will hurt you, I said,
and then we walked back.
Light in the garden end of Venice
kissed the Adriatic dusk good-night again
and pushed our moment east,
death at the end of a day
in love with your boy beauty.
I stretched the point
along some hidden line of cadency
and made you my descendant.

June 26, 2003
Langhorne

AN EXCEPTIONAL DAY
for RAP

Because you are an exceptional day,
when I go out in you
I am almost ashamed
of the boy I briefly become again in your light
this late clear afternoon of my life.

I remember the huge oak trees,
now gone, at Seventh Ward School,
sacrificed by architects
for a better view of the building
like the Aztec ephebe I stared at
in fifth grade in a *Geographic* layout,
his beating heart handed up to the gods.
And I know they will cut you down, too.

But in the meantime
as long as the four flashing
red tower lights are there every night in my dreams
you will be the man I never was,
no stranger to the day as I am,
to the sun, to where it comes from,
and to where we go from here.

YOUR HAIR

How does it come to curve
just there, just there and there?
Barely audible ringlets wave to me.

So it would grow for miles and miles,
so long as left untouched.

February 17, 1999

HOW LONG HAVE YOU BEEN?

Because somehow you have had news
that the world will never end
and do not know the lie
being young has told everyone
since childhood's invention;

   because you were told your days are long
with no urgent need to reply:

   because of your kind, slanted mouth
and square swinger's smile;

only a want of release is due
that must come now, come now,
come now, my darling,
and so, done come, so done.

You are relieved.
Here find the fresh splash
gasp enough to overleap the streets
wetted down like a film set
to make the image brighter.

We will wait for you,
suffer fondly,
fools of love.
There — the word — I said it,
there I said it,
quickly, gladly,
the longest word there is
that scares the biggest man,
the most seductive one

while you, friend,
manufacturer of desire
work overtime.

You liver of life
you heart and gut,
big feet, fingers spanning
through shocks of grassfield or hair,
parting the ways,
we look at each other
and you like one of Chillida's wind-combs
lunge blood, beating,
plunging into my brain's *sulci*
the *corpus cavernosum*
(better known as Plato's cave).
The wilding pulses,
globs aloft,
that keep you awake

dive into deeps,
fishers' bottoms, hunters' nights,
stars, invisible October clouds
all filled with coursing caution,
blood, lymph
starry ambergris,

ambush, sprays, groanings,
comings, goings,
and all of this in *your* good time.

Deadly deep like dear Walt's
wisdom-guarded nest,
your eggs draw up in a devil's chill,

your billion children swarming,
damned up in temperate silence.

I know that this is far from fair,
but I for one cannot pretend
I do not know
how life has lied to you
and what that does to me.

There is no sense in this
(another lie)
that we might give it
to make a way,
a way for you
and all the rest to come.

WHERE IT GOES, WHAT IT COMES TO
for M.G.

"O love, how did you get *here*?"
– *Sylvia Plath, "Nick and the Candlestick"*

Towards the end,
the aides from Tender Loving Care
stole her costume jewelry
but left the first editions of cummings,
the score from Rachmaninov,
the Tchelichev,
even the drawing by Ripley
showing the close of winter
as the end of an extended Broadway run.

And when she died,
what became of me,
my voice, and the long look
that finally turned me on?
Like Britten's Polish Phaedrus,
when you go,
I go, too.

What remained of her
was the serious black wood,
three sleigh bells on the inside door,
always warped,
a leaning hitching post,
a recipe for English Monkey.

I COULD BE NEAR

You had the window,
I the aisle,
an indivisible stranger
between us.
I saw I was near
and longed far off.
I did not peer,
since I could tell
that to be seen in men's eyes
was like a glancing blow to you.
I saw each gazing burned you
when your image cleared,
and so I chose the warmth instead
of some slight heat
that I could feel by staying very still.
It may well be
that heat is really heard
and looks can deafen judgment,
making every word
as monstrous as the siren sound
of a Manhattan ladder truck.
I only know that when I feel
and turn senseless,
when perception makes or meets
I don't know which perfection,
you could be near.

American Airlines, Flight 1800,
*   somewhere over Tennessee*
Late afternoon, Friday, November 12, 2004

SIGHED UNSEEN
for BG

Reduced to touching youth
with our eyes,
we know full well
the fathoming brain-betraying sneaks
that gazerape surface sight
and light upon the tactile organs themselves,
tactless and wild,
invasive, moist–
like your eyes,
my young friend,
that oversize your face.
I am here to see you.
That is my calling,
and so it seems there is
no other reason to be
on the scene
and not the seen.

Eyes do touch eyes after all
through the connective air
that lets it happen this way.
I lay my invisible hands of sight unseen
over that place
where the way into your mind
is as thin as your skin is pale.

Helpless, you brush it away
not knowing what you feel
praying over your face.
Light as shadow
grazing your hair

makes a direct hit.
You reel from the glancing blow
never to know what hit you.

The mystery solved,
the longing is over of me for you
when eye touching air,
touches eye.

THE KISS

In my mouth
where salt senses sweet
and bitterness seems transformed,
I am tasted,
and by some time magic
desire curdles the milk in me.
I cannot feed you any more.

I instead imbibe the bland
baby potion
of unflavored love
and drink it in
like a rhyming mariner's mirage,
blinding the horizon,
everything still between us.

HOW YOU KNOW YOU ARE IN LOVE

When you want to count the nape hairs
leaning over his collar
or comb the feather along his wrist.
Men must have walked
on the sides of their hands.

amo ergo sum

The lines of life are various; they diverge and cease
Like footpaths and the mountains' utmost ends.
— *Friedrich Hölderlin, "To Zimmer"* [1]

First-life's thoughtless tease
shows less by adding more,
and so stripped we grow,
sprouting flesh,
in-filling fortune's frame of possibilities,
revelation folding over girl or boy
who's first the neither one
we all were before.

Like you (since no one's special)
I, too, make fire from a little tinder,
tending to the inner burning,
tenderly tendering a swatch of flame
to anyone who would be brightened.

But then the wonder-censors come
and shame our senses' loud encounters
while little more we ask from them
than loving thunder
and standing in the rain,
if that is what we want.

The lines of life begin their meander
along our crowing eyes
and their distressing brow,
cheeks' scowl and laughter's streaks,
its furrows, the conduits of tears.

---

[1] Ernst Zimmer was an illiterate carpenter who looked after the great poet during his madness in a tiny attic room.

Outcropping crying laughs
sob our dry eyes
and so seduce us
we never really want
what we know.

The mechanism of flutters,
lashes, bats and winks,
tics and stares,
draws a bead on indecision.
We hide behind our eyes.

THEME FOR 206 VARIATIONS

I imagine the poem of your body.
The bones gone missing
hide with the boy in you.
I see what draws you
into its deeps.
Its passing we speak of,
we speak of discreetly.
Growth is a hardening
and first beauty is lost
in the body's coming together.
When touched it dies a bit
and you go slowly with it.
Saved from the seeing touch,
you survive. Never seen,
you outlive the liquid eye.

TO NO END

The marbled vein that runs
from the corner of your eye
into a dark, trimmed temple
pauses just long enough to reach out to me
as I strain to meet you there
at the squint. Both ways wander,
those guides to your intimacy
dangerously approaching affinity.

Like two lines often repeated
that famously, rarely, just barely never meet,
anatomy and I close in.

That swollen line comes of smiling, you know.
You, like all of us,
first existed thanks to a smile
and by returning it
started to pass it on.

Eye, vein, wrinkle form
unholy trinity
in the singular expression of your face.

Stay, sender of light-hearted speeches
and touching words not much spoken out
these days of unwinding spaces,
spincast Escher optics
and unshuttering sidelong glances
into the Where, with all its pressures,
postures, and mending promises.

Not a lot is much too tender,
so no more friendly feeling, please.
I pass on the gesture
(thank you very much),
the wink and smile.

TOPOLOGY

There is a young place
where the slouching body
folds not quite in half,
so lean that even air smiles at its lightness,
bends to its slightness,
trim against the wall,
its advocate and speech.
What holds it up?
The spare wish of hollow space?
A small loan past due
of green rectitude?
Empty like the ever-albino furrow
above the calf of someone kneeling,
long after a childhood on the beach
molding wet sand,
it wants to close
like a thick new book
opened in the middle
by a careless reader's incision.
It barely holds open.
Some would call the crease
a trope of weakness.
I would say instead
that in this miracle of all-color ease
the universe arches back onto itself
to where time begins
and a place for it is wanting.

MORE

Yet one more in the queue
with a crush on you
first gospel boy.
Spun of limerence,
you bear the wait and show
your longing, too.
You matter,
madness-maker,
who make my reaching
come full stop this time.
I want more.

Short Poems and Lyrics

THIS YEAR

Leaves getting smaller,
Lashes growing longer,

Fall closing darker,
Time makes me wander.

What bother, the anger!
Why posture and measure the other?

Fast pleasures follow.
No time to wonder.

EYES: FOUR LYRICS

- I -

In clouds raining on clouds
ice heals itself with water
that finally reaches earth.
Under the one wide-open sun,
Socrates' solar aperture is no eye
for his Alcibiades to gaze into.
The light that makes us see
first blinds us.

- II -

Night has the custom of waiting,
patiently staring
into another's eyes.
There is no secret,
only the fixing glance and gaze.

- III -

The sun returns in time.
It waits for the moon
to satisfy its boldness.

- IV -

Crowds of ice crystals
confound the site
of yet one more beginning.
Who can stand it?
The eye is closed to others' forbidding.

HAIKU

Sunrise on downtown
brick, slowly ripening orange.
A gray deafened cat.

DOMA HAIKU

Dry white April snow:
petals on gray Waverly
slate, heading on home.

19 April 2009

NO HAIKU

Sitting by the kitchen window
at one in the morning,
frost forms slowly
on the trunk lid of my neighbor's car,
parked there since last night.
Wisps of heat still rise
from the cooling engine.

SHORT OLD SONG

Ev'ry day
I hope the night
will come.

Yellow leaves
drop down
to sweep the street.

THE EVER SLOWER GOING OF THINGS
for MG

Things were going
so slowly,
so well,
I didn't hear the chime.
My namesake's mantle clock
rang the between times,
4 a.m., when it's neither
yesterday nor tomorrow.

WHEN YOUNG

When you're young
that's just about all you have to be,
but usually it's also all you are.
All, after all, is something, too.

OLD MEN ALONE

Begging for words
from anyone,
money means nothing.

TO LIFE

The only way to live with shame,
the price you pay for really seeing someone
other than yourself,
is to turn yourself in to time.
Give it up!
A warrant is out for your arrest.
Let them empty your pockets
for everyone to see
what you carried close.
Stand still for a headshot!

THE MUSE AT THE TABLE

The muse arrived at dinnertime
and found a place at table.
I offered it meat,
but it wants green.
I offered legume,
but it was full
of itself already.
It stayed for dessert.
I ate chocolate.

COMING TO MY SENSES

Your thin limning gestures,
past touching,
bound off my inner ear
that hears nothing
of your voice waving
back to me.

THE POET

The poet knows
how things are
better said
when better left
unsaid.

WHAT MAKES US DIFFICULT

What makes a poem difficult
is just what makes something
difficult for us: the pivot words
both and *and*.

WHERE TIME AND DESIRE CONVERSE IN RETURN FOR WAITING THREE MONTHS TO SEE YOU AGAIN

You're *beautiful*.
Now what?

Mothers and Fathers

THE FENCE
for JJ

The fence was secured,
the story goes,
between the final rows of stones
by grandpa and mortar
as a way to keep me safe
from rolling off the grass in fun
and over the wall
to the graveled driveway below
and certain death,
a concussion at least —
or was it an elbow bruised?

So began the mantra
"I musn't get hurt"
I grew up hearing
that kept me from roughhouse play and dirt
and asylum from other boys.

I hated that fence
of gas pipes and farm-field mesh.
Finally, the wall began to lean
away from the weight of years of morning glories,
rose bush roots and bales of peat moss,
the weight of rain,
and the inevitably shifting earth.

At five I escaped by the front steps
and later by car into adolescence,
and eventually on to New York.
Now that the guards have also gone on,
the home and grandma long since away,

the fence is finally down for good,
but far more has been broken than an arm
and never found the boys.

THE LAST PAIR

No one now to embarrass, I admit.
My mother bought my shoes
and sent them by mail
for twenty years
since nothing matched our tastes
in any other way.
Cordovan loafers,
burgundy Riva,
made in Bombay.
Years on end
she sent them,
wrapped in Christmas paper.
I'm wearing the last pair.

July 8, 2003

AND SO

... and so
alone at last,
so soon after all,
although I would not have thought
the time would pass this fast.

It bade release
and gave relief —
who would have known? —
and waved away the bitter time
that's now no better time
for the end of bother
than a half-century before.

My one mother —
suddened silence! —
who worried loneliness
more than any thing else,
left it and me
easily alone.

2003

THE CELL

Only one cell is the father's.
But everywhere in a man's body
it tastes the opening word.
It sees the high-speed road bearing down.
It lines the heart
and presses down with every step.
It's in the finger's whorl,
the iris' stars, the wandering vein.
It lifts and listens,
licks and smiles.
It bodies out each lash and nail,
and in our musty hair
it hides and smells.
The flexing knee,
the curling toe, the waving hand:
all are in daddy's code,
though grown and lost
and read and known.

March 2001

MY FATHER'S EYES

His fingernails are long by now,
much too long for his taste.
His five-o'clock shadow has lengthened,
too dark for him.
He always shaved.
But, oh, my father's blue eyes!
I wonder how they look
and what they see now
that so rarely looked at me.

HOW LITTLE I THOUGHT

How little I thought of myself,
how much about my self
till she who, burdened,
carried me to term
arrived at her own simple end.
One small outspoken breath
whispered her away,
the telling word unheard.
She entered on her own
and later set me on my way.
A little breeze later
and just that soon had passed.

eorthe weorold

The skin lies still,
dormant on latent, imprecise flesh,
a woman's arm and shifting parts–
leg, breast, the upper arm–
so many pieces from a box of toys
found in the hallway closet
assembled for serious games.

But something pushes up
like molten mineral love
against the single skin
of a young man's body,
its edgy terrain
a desert scene
of windblown flatlands
shifting tectonic plates beneath.

She, the first, is a settlement,
homestead, moist,
a founding thing
for foundlings and changelings,
a thing heavier than it looks,
at ease for fondling,
simply to be there, at rest.

The other-hand sex,
in fact the second
(Mme de Beauvoir *au contraire*),
under pressure to reach
to turrets and towers,
all rampart
with unexpected strain

announces the simple investiture
of upsurging awe to everyone
who has the heart to see,
and in terror of being still
then scares us away.

His flesh gleams
in its slow rising
like the shiny caul of proofing dough
for "a stabilized biofoam
of wheat endosperm,"
this bread of life.
Tidal blood pumps faster
in tribute to him
through a thousand striated courses,
returning to its sources
only for air.

All surface,
never seeming to tire
even at ease,
an always sparer frame
(of the gods) tenses,
making its landscape and firmament
tenseless,
all together at once.

And to think these things are
not much spoken any more.

Why do we then
fondly almost steal
looks away from stoic stretching,

the straining so taut as to seem insensate
and *not* to be desired?

At what a loss to a mother,
who cannot give him a way
to steel himself,
to be the ever after other
from a start in her indifference.
He is a primitivity
that runs and hides
from the source in her,
and ever on the run thereafter
an escapee from womanhood,
in hiding.

As much a loss to father, too,
who could not bear him then
nor can he now,
to recognize himself
in him, the boy,
who should be taken up
in rite, in celebration
of a being another
of father's own kind
and kindness.
But he like Abraham
denies the son his own selfsame
on loan from father's boyhood
to learn the world's invention,
manhood, "the big impossible,"
the unnatural complement
of what his mother earth

had made out of her deep ground,
and makes instead a sacrifice
of the both of them.

I see we have this something
wonderful to do with
as often as possible.
Hearth and we are old,
and never together.

BREASTS

When I think of breasts
I remember two old women upstairs
in our overheated attic on Victory Terrace,
dressing while I played on the floor,
the deep furrows across my Grandma's shoulders,
and the smell of stale Shalimar.
My father hated their presence there.
I now know why.

I was drawn by the scent
of those blue-veined monstrosities
that served insatiable bluebeards' interminable
babyhoods,
holding in their murky, viscous readiness
the mystery of superfluous tumescence,
a case for surplus and endless supply.

MY GRANDMOTHER

I remember my grandmother
bending to pick up bits of lint from the carpet
when a vacuum cleaner was just at hand.
Why renounce the convenience of a machine?
Did she want to touch the places we had walked on?
What was she reaching for
each time she bent down?

New York Poems

NEW YORK

I will one kite-perfect dusk in April
send myself out on a string,
push away the clouds
and free the sky
at thirty-thousand feet.

Guest in my heart,
the City lies below,
its crossings open to view
hiding the downtown streets.

A pilot voice says,
"Look what's left
of an unforgettable life."

I pull in the string,
cut the pressure lock,
and sail.

SIXTH AVENUE

Bodies harden.
The breeze stirs me.
I've been inside a long time
and half expected to find myself
on the skin of others.
Always saving,
I was starving.

All us loners,
older too soon,
feeling less
can only get younger.

I live in the groove,
never straying,
never stirring,
watchful waiting
bashful burning,
always naying,
never knowing.

July 1986

HAND ON THE SUBWAY CAR POLE

Just at the Canal Street jog
on a Red Line downtown express,
I wanted to take your pulse
(I would gladly have given it back)
to make some sense
of the minor blip
I saw above your thumb,
the telling arterial wink,
blood nod,
echo of your heart's
constant knock-knock who's there?
pressing to get out
above a freshly laundered
pristine cuff.

Your fierce, restless grip,
holds on for dear life this morning
and I see what gently brushed
against your lover's lash
as he slept this morning
when you left.

Fall 2002

111

THE TRAVELER

His hard face and fine eye,
fixed stern and impassive,
asleep in the morning,
is a baby's face.
Before leaving home
he practiced the look:
Don't mess with my business!
Don't touch!

But there, leaning back
on the Staten Island Ferry,
the clenched jaw relaxes,
the tough boy's chin hangs soft.
He might be Mother's little Oedipus.

I SHARE A YAWN WITH A PERFECT STRANGER

Two languid posers
riding ESCALATOR UP,
keeping the two-stair rule,
moving together,
staying apart.
He turns on his heel,
like a tree hell bent
against an early March wind.
We yawn like hungry nestlings,
mouths meet agape
across space,
eyes closed
in nothing-spoken eloquence.
Two perfect strangers,
we reach the top and disembark,
at one, just once, with one another
on the way to heaven.

Whitehall Terminal, April 1998

THE DEAD SQUIRREL

On this cold December day
a dead squirrel
is an especially pathetic thing.
Splayed on the wet walk
under a chestnut tree,
he still looks airborne.
Already, perhaps only hours
after his fall from grace,
the once meticulous fur
bristles into a sprig
of gray pine.

DARK BIRD
for Hitano MFM

i first saw you
more than thirty years ago
this time of year
in a heavy snow and as bitter cold
standing in the street
at Bedford and Carmine
bundled in a long heavy coat
dark like your hair
my christ! you're still here
or come again
you were far away in the blizzard
looking for drugs or a place to stay
i blamed the wind
for hiding your face
behind your hair
everyone walked slow steps
against my ally, the wind
even the taxis weren't running
the night before
i had looked down
on that very corner
from an illegal rooftop
at the edge of adolescence
now suddenly there was no wind
and the hair held onto your face
like a dozen bleeding worshiping
rhizome hands
guarding the crucified bones
under your eyes
by now i've unlearned as much as I need to know
and since you disappeared on me that day

i know less
thank heaven!
about corners and snow
but when you appeared again
oh jesus! i laughed like the believers
i danced with their cymbals and other instruments
and the words printed in red
on paper translucent as the skin on your face
purified by days of cold air
your impassive face on Prince Street
washed by more daylight
than i've seen in all the intervening years
since your first coming
into sight
after you left me tonight
to walk in the gardens of early night
i went to sobs about the dust
on Duchamp's broken glass
that moved you so much
who talks that way any more?

you see the Sixties were a dream
and since you've come back
living life harder than you have to
i look at you
but how can i believe?

perched like some dark bird
you whose "happiness is seeing
other people happy," you said
or the way you eat bad bread
from a Greek diner
with grace and gratitude
i was the host for what i knew

was our last dinner
under your stern Andalusian smile
prim lips when the angelus rang somewhere
you fed me one more bite
the blood returning
from feeding your hair
the vein on your forehead
a lightning flash when you laughed
me from your past,
come out you lover of the *kairos*
as it draws me on into the future
in that one starry instant breath before creation
you saw that places are things
the random light of everyday forgotten corners
the chancy shadow
emanating an invisible reflection
people stumbling passing you by
to whom you give in stern return
the prize of your notice and the thought
that here we are and this is it
as brother Alan said
what's what
no comings or goings
only *Gegenwart*
the spellbound moment
but can anyone be in it with you?

February 14, 2004

PEDAGOGUES

We are an occasional smooth stone
on the cliff face they must climb unattended.
We have been there, but know
few footholds among so many promises.

We are the stepmothers and missing fathers
they've clambered among along the way,
whom they must leave behind,
and leave without regret.

But how can we tell them
there are no guides among the starry orders,
no resting places,
and the way up is *not* the way down?
Sure of wonder, they grow suspicion
in the clear medium of their eyes.

CENTRAL AMERICA

Facing us, he displayed the Americas.
Turning, a bit of New Zealand
peeked out below the North Face
pack on his back.
Washings had dimmed the gray to a loose fit
and worn away great patches
of a *Geographic* appliqué.
Most of the contiguous States were gone.
Little was left of the heartland,
the Continental Divide,
Great Lakes, and vast weathery states.
Below his beltline,
the southern hemisphere.

As our train slowed in
to Union Square,
perhaps to steady himself
or comfort the disintegrating earth that covered
his body back and front,
he ran a single finger
along the equator
and the last particles of Central America,
somewhere near his navel,
fell away.

NEMO LEAVES UTOPIA
for mo'r(e)

Caution departs Penn Station at 4 a.m.
The bars close in on time,
on prisoners donning chic, wrinkled boredom,
and pale, dry, paper-thin caps.
He reaches for his lower east side.
Everything is as it was.
Nemo leaves Utopia.

WHAT I LEARNED FROM MY CAT
to Mr. E (1986-2003)

Watch the feet of human beings,
not their eyes.

The ears are erogenous zones.

Every body part is a toy.

It's OK to be alone
for long stretches of time.

Take many hours to groom.

One can be soft *and* fierce.

Never bark.

Always keep the toilet bowl clean.

Whisker my name daily,
quickly, softly:

Mr. E
Mr. E
Mr. E
Mr. E

Visions

ON LAUREL SUMMIT
(near Jennerstown, Pennsylvania)

Looking out across the stretch
on Laurel Summit
where rolling ridges fold together
in dark venous concourse
under a November day's rain-damp breath,
you see the Appalachian head thrown back,
his long Devonian throat is open,
exposed like an uprooted tree,
lying half buried by the weight of soughing air.
The blood of deep ground movement
rushes to his face, impending winter,
explodes in a gaze, upward bound.

TREE STANDING

Its trunk conceals a beating heart.
The solid pulse within is firm and strong.
High wind fails to break the shaft of thought
that holds its torso up
to question the roam of reason and talk.

On top, a poem issues out
from fingers flickering green,
fussing with the light,
as night wishes in toward the trees
that understand our way.
Someone, you know, is dying now.

March 8, 2001

THE IMAGE LOVER

Open night,
I was your lover.
I follow rivers.
The image hovers.

Late at night,
I come upon you.
With this sign of you
I cast my light.

I was your lover.
What did you see?
Time has lapsed.
I follow rivers.
The image hovers.

FEAR OF EYES

What is the fear of eyes?
Bits of brain stalking the earth
that want your words, your name.
They stun, cause cower.
Infants gape and reach for their blink.

Who is in there?
Twin moony faces posing as me.

Long stares draw fire.
Drink to me only tastes of blood.
Is everything finally
something to eat?

STOPPING LOOKING

I have stopped looking.
Will I now be seen?

What does the eye see?
What is *there* to be seen?

The eye as blind as Tiresias'
drinks in light.

One looks to Venus,
the other Mars.

You do not see me.
Who is looking?

You with perfect lucent eyes
who do not look at me,

you who do not see me,
lover of eyes, I know you.

Insight fails this visionary.
There's nothing more to see.

In the glare of glance to staring glance
we look away.

The I fails to focus,
nearer than we think.

For our sere blindness
we have eyes because we see.

SHADOWS ARE THE SIGNS OF LIGHT
(in memoriam *James Agee*)

The shadows cast by high-flying planes,
fabulously small,
 fall across me.

I sit in the heat a high summer day,
 scouting the sky for signs
  and terrors.

Brief dusks of low-flying birds,
 asking to be read,
  flash by.

CENTAUR, MID-DAY

It comes to be with her,
giving down
as quiet as late spring wind.

Crazy persistent birds
call it on,
rain releasing the green.

The presencing centaur arrives
contending
the connective air.

A slight yellow fuss of new willows pauses
coming out of cloud,
a single unforgettable new leaf shudder.

MIDSUMMER

And if I needed
to end midsummer
with someone
and see him again,
it would be Billy Budd
the dancer,
"his welkin eyes expanding,"
who taps his boots on woodsedge,
where Kleist's marionettes
walk round at dawn.

CLOUDS

These clouds are mine
like the birds we kids called for:
"My money! My money!"
The rest is hidden.
Such clouds are hands
passing under one another
in steady unfolding.
They do not touch,
they do not join.

ECLIPSE

In the starscape
is a face I have seen once only,
the same ironic eyes
of everyone I've ever seen
and one I've surely not seen.
How simple it must be
to understand the stars.

MILLIONS OF AUREOLES

Millions of aureoles
sudden moves
felled trees
broken words
done deeds.

Half as many navels
happy trails
wishes
handfuls of charms.

November 30, 1999

SUMMER'S RESEEDING
(Waverly Place at Bank Street)

Soon summer reseeds,
its light dry powder petals
the bleached green answer
to early spring's blossom drifts.
Handfuls of feather-light dust
blow back in advance
of autumn's flowers falling
like crumbs cornered in a broken bread box
or wedding rice left behind in the cracks of a sidewalk.
Too early for hiding, storing, saving.
Too late for planting, waiting.

A GUEST BETWEEN

I'm well when the weather's mean
on a gray-souled November day
or summer solstice, say,
strawberry moon impending.
But now that it's nice
it makes me sick to think.
Thoughts that send me roaming
break my slipping stride,
careful steps now hardly heard,
still undetected.
I pull back,
tramping down
what brings my life to me.
Where was I roaming?
The joy is there in possibility,
up close to the where and the when,
on Hölderlin's distant peaks
and we the abyss between.

CREDITS

Rolling up as the film unwinds
its last few hundred turns,
a few of us sit through the credits
waiting for the mnemic epilogue
we went there
to find in the dark.
Each second memory
enters in the twenty-fifth frame.

CRUSHES

There are the crushes of people
warning their way, unwilling *frotteurs*
with effortful disinterest lurching in failure
to find yet another no place,
here against her swollen bag,
his black carry-on,
the gangster's pocketed gun,
the heavy-scented hint of menstrual flow.

And then there are the crushes
for those who love to tongue
drab sugar-clogged phantom-colored slop
from infantile margaritaville
till everything tastes of metal.

Do not forget the crush of bone into flesh
and pure feeling by mangling machinery,
La Mettrie's beautiful cage
in which we are trapped for life,
now macerated, mashed, contused,
and smothered in pain
by a growl of release
till the numbing oxytocic damp arrives.
Such cuts short all dancing.

And last now
the crush of my dear you
whom I welcome.
Like all three:
unwanted, sweet, disabling.

RECIPE: FOOD FOR DREAMS

Precisely at ten p.m.,
take a handful of oats,
overwhelm them with water,
add a spot of milk, sixteen raisins,
and nuke it all
for as many minutes as there are raisins.

Somehow tonight, however,
it occurred to me that
putting the hot pyrex bowl
on her monogrammed throws
would be like pressing
the invisibly hot glass
against my mother's skin.

Each folded three times
I move the first throw on top,
then the other layered under it
and rest my now warm goodnight
on the bedspread underneath,
not too many, not too few.

DESERT LANDSCAPE

Settled contours
stretch out before me
against desire's horizon,

pressured by weather-shaped winds
and burning weeks
to yield its inner shape.

A hidden bloodforce sea
holds me firm,
mimicking Phidian form, unyielding.

THE GREAT WALL

Beauty is a monumental wall,
the edifice of every story

built of eyes passing judgment
on we who see,

on hands that wary off,
dismiss and wave away.

And closing in on being—
just this close—

beauty's split-second absence,
transparency keen to delight,

clear to love, stares back at us
who never wished to look.

THE HALF-LIFE OF DYING

What really kills us, it seems,
what does us in
is others' dyings
and their getting there.
We see for them
in our waiting,
wondering how we will feel.
Like radioactivity,
that finds its way
into our bones
to while away its half-life
until the osseous glass is full
and cannot take any more light,
dyings halve us again and again
until having enough,
we are emptied
of wondering and waiting,
whethering and whying,
with always one more to go.

THE PAST
for WJ

There is no past, young friend.
Whatever it is impassioned to be, I'm sure,
no one has ever known.
We see only the present perfect,
tense, perfectly present,
sliding along the blue road.
We leave nothing behind –
the country house,
a heavy, woman's table,
the biker in Trieste at 4 a.m.,
heavy rain in Colombi Park,
the road to Meßkirch.

Nothing is endless.
Nothing is over or lost.
Return to nostalgia?
The ache of what's coming
Is your precious prescience.

A messianic shivery blade
cuts the not of words
and talk of such a thing as the past
and sets it free
to drift through doings
and things not done,
making you leave for the future
on the next train
already in the station.

Never fear,
we never *were* here.
We are merely turning corners from nowhere
like the pages of an unfinished term paper
on madness and memory.
Without history and befores
there is no commitment,
precedent or promise,
no note left for later.

What remains, then, if nothing *is*?
Isn't all willing a happy end
to dead lines and universals,
creation *from* and making *for*?
Relative sleep conspires.

PROMISES

Words make no promises after all.
No more does
    a first red leaf make us its fall.
    Ahead, it's autumn.

A man who follows the rain
Invariably heads east.
    But is going back on his promise
    such an untoward, forward thing
    all the same?

THE MANY WAYS THE FACE

The many ways
the face faces us
hadn't fazed me till today.
Now I face the music,
and in and about
a light *volte-face*
I see him from his other side,
the side that leaves me alone
after decades.

That *facies* —
deceptive, decisive —
its spell has ended.
The smiling palindrome
looks away,
and I am free
to see him as he was.

A slight turn (imagine!)
and what once unmade me
makes me now
his echopraxia, a glance
(let's face it!)
down my way.

September 13, 2008
Café Doma

147